The Esoteric Path to a NEW LIFE

Vernon Howard

Guidebook

First Printing 1984
Second Printing 2000

New Life Foundation
PO Box 2230
Pine AZ 85544
(520) 476-3224

Website: www.anewlife.org
E-mail: info@anewlife.org

ISBN 0-911203-44-3

CONTENTS

Introduction

Let's begin our exploration with a story containing a valuable lesson.

A tourist was driving slowly down a narrow road in one of our national parks. While turning a sharp bend he met a park ranger who smiled as he walked over to the car. The ranger said, "Go back three miles and turn right at the cabin." "I'm sorry," apologized the tourist, "but I don't understand what you are talking about." The ranger nodded and explained, "I'm talking about the way out." Only then did it dawn on the tourist that he was lost. In some way he had wandered off the main highway. He thanked the ranger and turned the car around. *It's about a better way.*

What is this booklet all about? It is all about the way *out*. Millions of human beings want out, but don't know how to do it. You will learn how. You will discover the way out.

a lost tourist needs to stop and ask directions.

Self-Knowledge

It begins by an honest admission that our old ways don't work. It begins when we acknowledge that we are powerless over our problem, and we need to ask for help.

The Esoteric Path to a New Life

The very title of this booklet is a story in itself. The dictionary defines esotericism as secret knowledge, as wisdom possessed by only a few people within the inner circle. The aim of this booklet is to reveal these esoteric mysteries to *you*.

What will the Esoteric Path do for you? We will discover the complete answer as we proceed. However, we can now say it consists of a totally new way to go through life. It is a way of self-harmony, and therefore, of exterior harmony, for the inner determines the outer. It is a way of having no painful questions about anything, for self-insight clears away self-confusion. If all this sounds too good to be true, just wait.

Where does self-knowledge begin? The answer surprises most people. It begins by seeing how many difficulties we actually have. Look around at people. It is easy to see that most men and women have lost their way. Their days are an endless parade of disappointments and heartaches, anxiety toward the future, a thousand fears, including the fear of not succeeding or of not making good impressions on others.

This may seem like a negative start, but it is highly positive and intelligent. When a competent doctor examines a patient he wants to know what is wrong. That is the only way to provide the cure. Likewise, in our lives it is good to see what is undesirable, for that leads to new health.

However, the surface awareness of our difficulties is not enough. Millions of human beings sense that something is wrong, yet remain as they are. So special medicines are necessary. *Self-honesty* is one of them. A *persistent wish* to become another kind of person is another. *Receptivity* to esoteric truth is a third. A *willingness to change* what must be changed is powerful medicine. So is a *willingness to see ourselves* as we actually are, *not* as we imagine we are. Whoever starts with these powers is off to a fine start. He has already loosened a brick in his self-confining wall.

Perhaps an encouraging thought has come to you at this point. The path *is* open to those who do not know what to do, whose lives are confused and agitated, who have reached the end of all the roads that once seemed so promising. Do you see why this is true encouragement? It is because an admission of confusion is the beginning of clearness.

You see, this path is not for those who pretend to have the answers already. It is not for those who think happiness resides in worldly success. This way is for those who no longer want to *pretend* that all is well, for those who know that they do not know. They are the ones who finally learn what it means to be truly free and happy human beings.

I would like you to please keep the next point in mind at all times. These ideas and procedures may seem unusual or even strange to you at first. They may sound contrary to what you presently accept as true. This is perfectly normal and is an essential part of the learning process. You can use it for inner advancement by simply observing your surprise or wonderment at a new idea.

Do just that much for now. Observe your reaction and let it pass from your mind, just as you might observe a bird passing and disappearing across the sky. Ask yourself, "Have my old ways and my usual procedures done anything for me?" Answer frankly. This provides fresh strength for abandoning the familiar but useless, in favor of the new and the productive.

Recognizing Psychic Sleep

We will now proceed step by step to examine the highly practical teaching of Esoteric Science.

Esoteric mysticism teaches that humanity dwells in a state of psychic sleep. It can be called by other names such as saying that man lives in foolish illusion. That he deceives himself about everything. That he lives in flattering and self-damaging ideas about himself and his life. This psychic sleep is the cause of every human problem and disaster. It is sleeping people who suffer from heartache and loneliness, from fear and violence. Only self-awakening can end these sorrows.

However, and please emphasize this point in your mind, _man does not know he is asleep._ So deep is his immersion in psychic hypnosis, that he instantly denies his actual condition. In other words, he does not know that he does not know. He spends his entire life under the gigantic illusion of being happy and productive, never once facing the terror in which he lives. Man huddles fearfully in a haunted house which he calls a castle.

Have you ever been in a room full of people when someone behaved foolishly or childishly? You sensed that he did not know how he appeared to others. In fact, he may have believed he was behaving cleverly or courageously. Everyone in the room saw him as he really was except the man himself. That is a perfect example of human hypnosis of psychic unawareness.

The ancient philosopher, <u>Socrates,</u> provided a classic illustration of man's mental sleep. He told about a group of men who were huddled together in a deep cave. Their only light was a fire that blazed in the center of the cavern. The fire cast strange shadows against the wall of the cave, frightening the prisoners. So the men sat there in terror and confusion. All but one. One of the prisoners made up his mind to explore the cave. When doing so, he found a secret tunnel. Following it all the way, he finally found himself in the outer world of sunshine and beauty.

We will now look at a chief characteristic of spiritual sleep. When this is understood all the pieces of life fall into place, revealing the whole picture. <u>Man has a false idea of who he is.</u> He has an <u>illusory sense of identity.</u> This false self is manufactured out of self-flattering imaginations and out of self-pleasing labels. <u>He labels himself</u> as a successful man, or as an intelligent thinker, or as a human being with lofty motives, but these are mere *ideas* he has about himself, and he is *not* these ideas.

We can easily prove this. Whenever a man feels depressed or irritated it is simply because his false identity seems not to be confirmed. Both these reactions are false, so the man is their slave.

Have you ever noticed how ~~nervous~~ *disturbed* people get when their pet ideas are challenged? Let this be a clue for you. By patient self-investigation we discover who we *are not,* and that ends the anxiety of not knowing who we are.

People identify with their thoughts and ideas.

To summarize this vital point, man wrongly believes that he possesses a separate self, an individual ego. This false idea causes fear, loneliness, neurosis. It throws him into conflict with other people who are also under the illusion of having separate selves. No man is apart from the whole—from the All. Man is one with the universe. Human beings are like dozens of ponds, each reflecting the light from the same moon. This is not philosophy, this is fact.

we are not our thoughts.
We dont own our thoughts.

It is very important, however, that we keep firm borders around our selves.

The Secret of Self-Observation

In serious moments people ask themselves, "Who am I? What is life all about? How can I have a truly meaningful life?"

The answer is, we must learn how to become one with ourselves, to separate the actual from the image, to awaken from psychic sleep. You are now ready to hear about your first step for doing just this.

Starting today begin to observe yourself in action. Whether you conduct business, or work in the home, or talk with a neighbor, whatever you do, watch yourself doing it. Alert self-observation is your first technique for self-awakening.

Here is a specific example. Right now, as you are reading this, notice your physical self. What is the position of your hands? Are your muscles unnecessarily tense? Be aware of the expression on your face. See everything possible about your physical self.

At the start, it is easier to become aware of physical items, but proceed from the outer to the inner. Observe the thoughts that pass through your mind when watching the news on television. Be conscious of the emotions you feel when criticized by someone.

Neither condemn nor approve *anything* you see in yourself. Just casually and impartially watch whatever is there. Reveal yourself to yourself. This self-knowledge is power for self-change.

True Excitement Is Finding Yourself

You know, people are always seeking a new excitement, a fresh stimulation, anything at all to push back the boredom and dreariness of their daily lives. They end up frustrated when denied what they want. Or, once getting their desire, they no longer want it. They are like guests at an exciting party who anxiously sense they must soon return to their unhappy homes.

You can be totally different. You can have an excitement that never swings over to depression. It is the true excitement of finding yourself. *Nothing* is more exciting than to watch a fear fade from the mind forever. Nothing is more delightful than to possess self-command in a world of chaos. There is no greater inspiration than to know that you have found the true path at last.

Live Life from the Present Moment

A primary aim of esoteric science is to guide man upward toward an entirely new way of thinking. Because this new way contains no pretenses and no contradictions, it produces ease and naturalness in whoever adopts it.

Preliminary progress consists of seeing that the present mind is *not* free of its self-defeating operations. One of its wrong moves is to interpret new ideas according to old thinking patterns. The story is told of a rabbit who is offered a bar of gold. The rabbit asked, "Where did you get such an unusual carrot?"

An unawakened mind sees everything according to its past experiences, according to personal preference.

Our task is to *not* live from a memorized plan of life but within the present moment. Only in the light of *right now* can we see things as they really are, and what we see is pure gold. So the first thing to realize about the human mind is that it is thoroughly conditioned. This means that it has been influenced and shaped since the day of birth.

Over the years a man collects hundreds of ideas about life and about himself. He gathers opinions about religion and philosophy. He stores up attitudes toward other people. He learns fixed methods for responding to events. By repeating the same thoughts and actions over and over, they become hardened within his mind. Then, feeling comfortable with them, he is very reluctant to replace them. No matter how wrong or how damaging an idea may be, the last thing he will do is give it up in favor of reality.

psycho sclerosis

When you speak to such a man about higher truths, he cannot comprehend them. Then, not comprehending, he either scorns or distorts the offered truth.

An ancient proverb points out that you can't talk to a summer insect about ice. The very awareness of our mental conditioning will help us break it. *Awareness is everything.*

Freedom from Life's Battle

Why do we wear ourselves out in battling life? Because we think we have enemies. Why do we think so? Because we unnecessarily dwell in the part of the mind which divides everything into opposites, such as: enemy and friend, inferior and superior, failure and success. But there is another way of thinking which dwells above all opposites.

This new way can be called consciousness, awareness, unconditioned perception, union with Truth—or it need not be called anything at all. In this state, there is no anxious need to have either enemies or friends, for you rest within the friendliness of your own original and free nature.

no, we still have enemies.

If a person writing a letter misspells a word, the error starts in the mind after which

Think of a grade school pupil.

it appears on paper. He cannot possibly correct the paper until the mind is corrected first. If he does not clarify his mind, the error must repeat itself on paper endlessly. No doubt you see the parallel here with human problems.

People try to correct exterior mistakes instead of correcting the way they think, which leaves them still chained to a mistake-making machine. The Esoteric Path emphasizes the need for clear thinking. For example, a healthy use of curiosity is to ask, "Exactly what will happen to me if I permit myself to see that I was wrong?" The answer is, *something good will happen.*

There is a part of your mind which is perfectly capable of standing aside to calmly observe another part which is disturbed. It is like a referee at a football game who sees everything, but is not involved in the battle.

Realizing this is one of the greatest discoveries we can make. You can see why. It proves the existence of another way of thinking, of a force which is never drawn

Trying to correct the outer will not work until the inner is corrected.

into the whirlpool of agitated thought. You will recall that we have called this the technique of self-observation. But, of course, we must practice until we experience this power for ourselves. Any daily challenge will serve.

Maybe you feel mistreated by someone. In this case, stand apart from your agitated feelings and watch how you feel. Just watch. Never mind if nothing happens at first, you're still experimenting. Quietly observe every upset feeling the moment it arises. What results from this? What results is a human being who is no longer the victim of exterior influences, a person who determines his own thoughts and who lives his own life.

Feel New Power and Energy

The natural power of electricity always existed, needing only man's discovery and application. Likewise, natural cosmic power exists within you at this very moment. Even as you read these lines, it awaits your recognition. It starts with self-study.

A common misplacement of psychic power is to wonder how long it will take to experience uplifting self-change. That only wastes valuable energy. It is not time that counts, but earnest intention. One good intention is worth ten years of curiosity about psychic growth. The earnest man detects small but definite changes very soon.

We need not seek some strange and mystical experience in order to enter the flow of authentic power. We need only think of negative states as being useless and unnecessary. For example, forcing is useless, unhappiness is unnecessary.

Simply proceed with the fact that inner warfare need not be bitterly endured, that it can be understood and ended. That procedure is fresh power in itself. To be conscientious in any endeavor is commendable, but it is indispensable to whoever wants out. So whenever you have a problem or need to achieve something, ask yourself, "What is the right procedure from the viewpoint of esoteric fact?" Like a bugle call, this alerts your psychic forces and places them at your service.

Right now, at this very moment, take a new interest in your life. You see, by an incredible fault in human nature a person can have great *concern* over his life without having any real *interest* in it. There is considerable difference between anxious concern and practical interest. The concerned man wants to protect his foolish self-images at *any* cost, while the interested man wants to destroy them *regardless* of cost.

People waste vast amounts of energy trying to please other people. Have you ever noticed how hard people try to please others by giving gifts and by saying the right things? Of course, very often the motive of the giver is to make sure that the pleased person is pleased with the giver. This is an example of *misused psychic energy*. Nothing good can ever come from pleasing people in order to make them pleased with us. A man becomes the slave of people whom he tries to please in the wrong ways.

So, spend your energies wisely. I will show you one way to do this. How rarely it occurs to anyone to try to please the only thing worth pleasing, which is the Kingdom of Truth within.

Let this idea dominate you. Ask the question, "What pleases the truth within?" The answer will arise from within. Truth is pleased whenever we welcome it, whenever we prefer *it* over illusion. Truth is pleased by our daily attempts to understand the principles which baffle us at first.

Truth is especially pleased by our admission that we have *not* been thinking for ourselves, for that opens the door to independent thinking. Truth is pleased by all such procedures, which anyone can begin and can maintain.

Live a Practical New Life

We have seen that the esoteric path is purely practical. Let's make that much stronger by saying that it is the *only* practical way to go through life. What is more practical than the ability to handle every daily event with calm efficiency? We will now discover how this is accomplished.

First of all, remind yourself that your adventure is an inward one. Do not try to change the external world. Change your own attitudes and viewpoints. When you change yourself, you change the world as far as you are concerned—for you *are* your own world. The interior and exterior are the same. Make this exciting discovery, for then you will see how it is perfectly possible to live in a confused society while remaining untouched by its chaos.

Take a simple example. You want something from another person. Let's say you want him or her to behave in a way which pleases you, but then this person does not behave according to your desire. All right, stop right here for a moment. Who has the problem? *You* do. Why do you have it? Listen to the principles of higher truth and they will say, "You have the problem because in your insecurity, you wish the other person's behavior to make you feel better." However, it is an illusion that another person can provide you with happiness.

Happiness is not the acquisition of anything—it is the *understanding* of something. So what must we understand? We must see that dependency breeds fear, not security. Seeing that, we cease to insist that others behave as we wish them to behave.

Whenever we have a demand toward another person, we are the slave of that person. Besides, even when a man gets what he wants from another person, he is never satisfied with it. He is compelled to demand more. Demands always fall into a bottomless basket, and the effort to fill the basket can only result in frustrating exhaustion.

Do you know anyone who lives like this? Stop for a moment and ask yourself, "How would my life be different if I had no fear of rejection by others?" Think about it. That freedom can be yours.

Let's discuss rejection in the light of

what we have learned. Our rejection by another person causes pain because of our unconscious *use* of the other person in maintaining unrealistic images about ourselves. We imagine ourselves secure, comfortable, loved and so on. Rejection exposes the image, shockingly throwing us back on our actual state of insecurity. But the shock is an *opportunity*. By bravely remaining with the exposure, by not trying to repair it with the glue of anger or panic, Reality then enters, which is our *total security*.

Escape the Prison of Illusion

The esoteric path leads us far beyond shallow words and slogans and propaganda. Words must not be taken as realities. Hearing the description of a beautiful countryside is not the same as *living* in that countryside. Which would you rather have: a description of a country home or the actual home?

Because they fail to see through words and labels, human beings live in mere descriptions of the good life never really seeing how little they have of it.

Take the word *freedom*. How frequently and how loosely it is tossed around by those dwelling in dreamland. We hear talk about political freedom, freedom from society's foolish rules, freedom from poverty and so on. But authentic freedom consists of just *one* state. That state consists of individual liberty from one's own *illusions*.

A person can have physical freedom or freedom from poverty and still be a slave to himself. So every man or woman must ask the challenging question, "What is my actual inner condition?" Ask that question of yourself. Ask it with a strong determination to see your actual condition, *whatever* it might be.

Is an envious man a free man, or is he in mental prison? Is a bitter woman at liberty, or is she behind invisible bars? See how simple the question is. The very examination of one's inner state begins to weaken whatever bars may be seen. This is the dynamic principle of self-honesty at work. Now you see the nature of authentic freedom. It is liberty from negative emotions, especially those we hide from ourselves. It is freedom from compulsive desires and false ambitions. It is true freedom when you are not torn this way and that by conflicting desires, but are one with yourself. It is true liberty when one is an awakened human being. And to be awakened is to be a *sane* and a *decent* human being.

Know the Truth When You Hear It

Never hesitate to bring a secret perplexity out into the open parts of your mind. Nothing harmful can *ever* come of it. To the contrary, good alone can result. For instance, you may exclaim, "But there are so many teachers and organizations offering solutions. How can I tell who is right and who is wrong? My bewilderment is doubled by seeing that one group teaches the exact opposite of another group. How can I separate the true from the false?"

There is a way to have perfect judgment. Doubt will disappear forever. You will be able to tell by a single glance at a teacher's face or by reading a single line from a book, whether or not you are being told the truth. The method is both simple and yet challenging. It is simply this: You yourself must prefer the truth above that which merely pleases you or which agrees with what you already believe.

Let's say the same thing in another way. By preferring that which is true and right for you, all that is untrue and wrong will fade away of itself. It is like hanging a wet coat out into the sunshine. The natural warmth of the sun evaporates the water, making your coat comfortable once more. But first you had to hang it out into the sunshine.

Whoever you may be reading this, there is something within you that knows the truth when it hears it. This does not mean that we always *choose* the truth, it means we *know* it. Our aim is to increasingly *choose* what we *know*.

Probably at one time you have been listening to music when the musician struck a wrong note. Instantly and without thinking about it, you knew the note was wrong. How did you know? Because you also knew harmonious notes when you heard them. Just as you have musical judgment, you also have spiritual judgment which can change a life of discord into a life of harmony.

Learning to Make the Right Response

Remember the importance of right responses. Right reactions to daily challenges can change the kind of day you experience. If hurt or upset by an event, say to yourself, "There is something here I do not understand as yet. I am capable of winning the needed insight and will search until it is won." When saying this, you are stating one of the cheerful facts of the esoteric path.

Picture a guard standing at the entrance of a factory which is developing a secret project. The guard's duty is to keep out spies and other unauthorized people. Now, as long as the guard remains alert and conscientious, as long as he performs his duty rightly, no harm can come to the project. Only if he wanders away or gets careless can anything go wrong. In other words, the guard needs only to stand where he is supposed to be standing.

This is how you can keep everything going right in your life regardless of how threatening it seems at times. All you need to do is stand in the right place. The right place is the site of esoteric wisdom. Make it your delightful duty to stand more and more faithfully in the right place every day.

Here is a principle which will keep you standing in the right place. Whenever you do not know what to do about something, simply be *aware* that you do not know, and *do nothing else*. Be aware of your condition, perhaps agitation or displeasure, and stop right there. Never mind if this does not seem like the right response. Never mind if you can't see how this can solve that financial problem or that domestic difficulty.

Unawareness of the whole picture is the only problem, so awareness is the only right action. Prove its rightness for yourself.

You need not surrender to anything negative — not to *anything*. You need not surrender to a secret and harmful habit, not to the trembling feeling of being at the mercy of people and events, not to impulsive actions which are later regretted, not to the dread that something bad is always about to happen, not to the fear that life is a losing battle.

No other human being can have threatening power over you unless your own fear gives him that power. Remember that. Anytime you wish, you can calmly refuse to be afraid of another person and that quiet refusal will end all fear. The fear is in *you* — not in his power, which is false power. Your enlightened mind has total authority over another person's unhealthy mind. And if he tries to make you afraid, he does have an unhealthy mind.

We must learn to listen to the voice of

reality, not to the voice of our own fears. To do this we must distinguish between reality and fear. To do *this,* we must become mentally silent—very silent. From this quietness there arises a unique realization. We see that fears are not a fixed feature of our psychic system, as we formerly imagined, but are foreign intruders having no real claim on us. By remaining alert to this reality, we easily dissolve all fears the moment they try to intrude upon our peace of mind. Your real nature cannot be hurt, or insulted, or rejected, or depressed by anything at all.

Imagine yourself standing in your home while pointing a flashlight's beam outside and into a stormy night. The storm has no power whatever to disturb the beam of light. Being of a totally different nature than the storm, the light passes through just as if the storm was not there. When our nature becomes different, storms may rage but they cannot touch us. You are then *in* the world, but not *of* it.

Command Your Life in the Right Way

People want to know how to understand and control daily events. It is quite possible to understand and command both events and people. However, this control is totally different from what people think it is. You must see control from the esoteric viewpoint, which we will now discuss.

You take command of everything in your day by having no need to command it at all. It is very important to grasp the meaning of this, so please follow and review carefully.

First, let's see why a man wants to control and influence another person. He may hope for a material advantage, such as money. But there is a deeper motive, a dangerously self-defeating motive. By having power over others, he thinks it confirms his possession of a separate ego, a separate self —for where there is the commanded, there must also be the commander. So in order to preserve the illusion of being a commander, he seeks every opportunity to control and influence people and events. But since he does not, in reality, possess a separate self, the whole show is a tragic delusion. Sooner or later the curtain must come down on the actor, leaving him frightened and lonely.

See through the illusion of having a separate self and you will then see there is no need to command anyone or anything. There is no such thing as you *and* a world to command. The world is what you perceive —and no more. Just command yourself and you command the entire world, for you *are* your world. This is oneness, this is self-unity.

To review, you command your entire day by having no false needs to have power over anyone or anything. <u>A man who is not in prison has no need to influence people who are.</u> In this state of self-unity, we then meet every daily event perfectly—whether it is a family situation, a problem regarding sex or any other challenge.

Helpful Hints for Self-Teaching

By this time you realize what is the most valuable kind of teaching: *Self-teaching*. While having the assistance of classes and books, <u>we must always end up as self-instructors.</u> The purpose of a class or a book is to help you to find your own resources of wisdom, to guide you toward being your *own* guide.

Let's take an example of a man we will call Mr. X. Mr. X no longer wants to live with feelings of emptiness. Moreover, he is tired of pretending to himself and to others that he is on the winning side. Though successful according to society's standards of success, a feeling of futility has taken him over. How might Mr. X teach himself?

He could say something like this to himself, "I have brought my feelings of futility up from the cellar of my mind to where I can see them clearly. Of course, it is a bit uncomfortable to realize that a sense of futility was there all along, but this is a good and healthy forward step. For the first time I see that a person can be successful as a businessman or as a husband, and yet be a failure as a human being. I want to be inwardly successful, for I sense that this kind of success is all that really matters."

A woman named Mrs. Y can be our next example. Though in the same rocking boat as Mr. X, she occupies a different corner. Every day she is overwhelmed by painful and perplexing emotions. She feels like a stick in a raging stream that falls into one whirlpool after another. Mrs. Y could begin her program of self-instruction by saying, "I sense clearly that something is wrong with my life in general and with my emotions in particular. I'm easily offended, quickly defensive, frequently nervous. Esoteric teachings say that this agitation can be conquered by studying truthful principles. My part is to listen and to learn, so that is what I will do from now on. I do not want to continue with my old ways, for their satisfaction was a hoax."

Some Questions You Might Ask

At this point I will answer questions typical of those asked at our classes:

Question 1: Man has tried thousands of schemes for establishing peace on earth, including religions and laws and peace organizations, but everything has failed. Why?

Answer: Why? Because unawakened men think they are awake. Unawakened men can do nothing but make the social system into what they are inwardly like. And inwardly they are lost. The inward duplicates itself outwardly. What man calls social improvement is merely a new arrangement of the old chaos. It is like a man who moves from one part of a jungle to another part, but deludes himself by calling it a new paradise. Society is not going to change, but through sincere self-work any individual can transform himself. Remember, if you choose to remain in the psychological jungle inhabited by society, you will have to suffer as society suffers. You need not do so.

Question 2: You have urged us to see ourselves as we are, not as we like to picture ourselves. What are most people like?

Answer: Like a thermometer. Their feelings rise or fall according to the social atmosphere. Never living from themselves, they remain at the mercy of exterior events. Everything outside tells them how to feel inside. They are slaves to bad news, or an angry look, or an unexpected change of plans. And, of course, the more a man is influenced by exterior events, the more he will angrily insist that no one tells him what to do. It is not necessary to live like a mindless thermometer. Any man can learn to live from himself.

Question 3: What determines our rate of speed along the esoteric path? Maybe I can state the question in another way. How can we make swift progress toward self-unity?

Answer: How much truth can you take without getting irritated or distressed? That is what determines your progress. The more you can take, the faster and higher you can climb. Remember, irritation and distress tell a lot about your psychological level. Happily, the more you take, the more you are able to take. So even if you react wrongly to a truth you don't want to hear, try to observe your reaction. Be aware of your resistance. This awareness will make you more receptive, which is the same as being on a higher level of understanding. While it may seem otherwise at times, nothing but good can come from courageously hearing the truth that parts of us do not want to hear.

Question 4: Why are personal problems so persistent? Even when one of them goes away two more jump up. What is wrong with our attempts to end problems?

Answer: Any attempt to solve a problem on the level of acquired thought can only sink us deeper into the problem, for conditioned thought *is* the problem. So we must see and practice the right way.

We must rise from the level of everyday thought to the higher level of consciousness. Consciousness is above the plane of battling thought, and therefore has *no* problems at all. The attempt to solve difficulties with acquired thought is frustrating escapism, but to use consciousness is wise self-elevation. Never mind if all this sounds strange to you. Give it your careful attention. Someday you will be very glad you did.

Question 5: What is an awakened man like?

Answer: We could talk about it for hours, but I will mention one characteristic of an awakened man. Having had the courage to examine his own nature, he understands the nature of other people. At a single glance he knows the psychological history of any man or woman he meets. This makes him very wise and practical in his relations with friends and strangers. No one can deceive him, for only a self-deceived man can be deceived by others. His knowledge of human nature is a

41

thousand miles above that of ordinary psychology. Because of this, he is the only kind of a man who can really guide human beings out of the jungle. But he also knows that the vast majority of human beings have no intention of ever leaving the jungle. He helps only those who want out, not those who want to argue.

Question 6: You have said that there are true rewards for the man or woman who walks the esoteric path. May we hear about one of them?

Answer: One reward is the ending of useless and tiring tasks. Have you ever noticed how many things you do which you secretly wish were out of your life? For example, do you know how much energy you waste in trying to make good impressions on people? And have you ever noticed your tension when wanting to make a favorable impression? That is a form of slavery seldom noticed by most people. You don't have to impress *any-one*. You need only be a *real person*.

Be Free of Painful Memories

The story is told about two disciples who were walking back to their school of esoteric truth. They came to a stream having no bridge. A woman was standing there who expressed her desire to cross the stream. One of the disciples promptly picked her up, waded through the water and set the woman down on the other side.

For the next several miles the helpful disciple was scolded by his companion. The angry friend accused, "As a disciple of higher truth, you had no business to even touch a woman." The helpful disciple finally turned to his irritated friend to say, "Look, I put that woman down an hour ago. *You* are still carrying her."

This illustrates one of the chains which binds most men and women. They are chained by time, by memories of the past. They are therefore tyrannized by thoughts about unwise actions of yesterday or they yearn for past days which seemed happier than today.

One of the great secrets of the esoteric path is your ability to escape from time. Certainly we use clock and calendar for practical purposes of everyday life. But we can be free of psychological time and live entirely in the present.

The present moment is totally free. So live *right now* without the interference of useless thoughts about past or future. That is how to live freely, spontaneously, naturally.

Lessons Others Can Teach Us

As you attend lectures and classes and as you mingle with people elsewhere, you have endless opportunities to observe all these human reactions. You should study people just as a scientist examines specimens in a laboratory. The study of other people helps you understand yourself. Also, self-study reveals the motives and desires of others.

Let's take a practical example of this.

Suppose you meet someone who has a severe emotional problem. Now, you must never permit the problem that another person has with himself to become *your* problem. In many cases the troubled person will try to involve you in one way or another. He might insist that you owe him your attention or your time or your money. In order to get what he wants from you, he may try to make you feel guilty. Don't feel guilty. Stay uninvolved.

You will eventually see that this is not selfishness on your part and it is not a lack of compassion. It is the dawn of a new understanding of a certain cosmic law. That cosmic law declares that every man is responsible for his own rescue. The man who falls into a pit is the *only* man who can climb out of it. Besides, when you try to help a man who rejects the truth, you only make him worse.

Remember, a person who is right within himself always knows just what to do and just what not to do in his relations with other people. Just as we forecast a storm by knowing clouds and temperature, so can we forecast and avoid psychic storms by knowing how human nature operates in its depths.

Learn to Look in the Right Place

In order to illustrate a basic truth about life, ancient philosophers told a story about the astronomer and the stars. The astronomer habitually took an evening stroll outside the city to gaze at the starry heavens. While lost in stargazing, he fell into a well. His cries for help brought rescuers on the run. One of them advised, "It is better to see your very next step than to lose yourself in skies you do not as yet understand."

The keys to right living are as close as your own mind. To look in the direction of human rules is to stumble and get hurt, which happens to millions of people every day. But the mind that has wandered from itself can also return to itself, and then there are no more questions.

If we are confused about cosmic matters, we will also be confused about earthly affairs. But clarity on the cosmic level provides awareness on the human plane. It is useless to try to understand human affairs as if they are apart from cosmic action. We cannot understand a flying stone just by watching its flight. We must see who threw it and why.

A man understands why his life unfolds as it does by understanding the operations of his own nature. He must understand that *he* is the cause of his own effects. Not only does he get what he gives, but he gets what he *is,* for like attracts like. An eagle is attracted to another eagle. A sheep desires the company of other sheep. In other words, a man attracts to himself more of what he already is. This cosmic law operates endlessly, whether or not the man understands it. He must seek to understand.

This information is a delightful revelation to those who no longer want to attract unhappy results. They can study themselves and change their nature, after which different and happy results are certain.

For the next several days do this. Observe how a thought produces a certain kind of result. Notice that an excited thought reproduces the excitement in your voice or in gestures. Observe how a gloomy thought spoken aloud to another person tends to make the other person gloomy.

This practice helps you to understand the mental law of cause and effect. You then understand that you can change your life by changing your thoughts.

You Can Know the Right Thing to Do

People constantly cry out, "But what shall I do?" The answer is that you have nothing to do but be yourself, which means to stop being the stranger that goes around masquerading as you and spilling you into one heartache after another.

If you could see the full significance of this statement, you would know just what to do when someone offends you, when you are afraid of being alone, when you feel lost and helpless.

When you are yourself, the question of what to do will never arise, you simply flow. In this free flowing there is no separation between you and whatever comes your way. Because you are one with all of life, there is nothing to question, nothing to decide, nothing to fight. In this state of understanding the entire world is yours.

The world is your classroom. Use it as such. Observe how anxiety and confusion dominate the people you know. Then notice how unhappiness and pretense go together. Then see even deeper. See that unhappy people live in pretense because they don't know what else to do. They actually believe that pretense is essential to their survival.

The fact is, pretense is just another prison bar preventing wholeness. The very awareness of this is an invitation to wholeness.

Take self-contradictions in people. You have noticed many times how people say one thing while thinking another. This is a simple example of psychic self-division. A man says he is glad to help his neighbor, yet feels resentful when called upon for aid. If he had no false sense of duty toward his neighbor, he would not trap himself like that.

Self-insight ends a false sense of responsibility toward others and, therefore, frees you from guilt. Your first duty in life is toward your own self-awakening, so never permit self-centered people to make demands upon you. Two sick people can't help each other, but if one of them gets well he can be of genuine help to the other. Self-healing comes first. *Make* it first.

We have seen that another psychic world exists. We have also seen your ability to dwell in its richness. A third point must be made. This new world can be reached by only one path. That path is to apply esoteric truths to our inner nature, to make them a part of the daily self. We must receive and hold truthful impressions, much like the basin around a tree receives and holds water. That is what succeeds when all else fails.

Guidelines for Your Journey

Here are two actions which will make this guidebook of maximum benefit to you:

Action 1: Read this as often as possible. Each time try to see a new truth or lesson not seen before. You will be pleasantly surprised at the speed with which everything becomes clear. By working in your own orchard, you receive the fruits of that orchard.

Action 2: Join a study group or form your own group for esoteric exploration. Great energy is awakened when earnest men and women meet for the purpose of inner enlightenment.

We will now summarize everything we have covered by reviewing twelve outstanding points.

1. Mankind dwells in a peculiar state of spiritual sleep, which causes all his heartaches and tragedies. However, any sincere individual can awaken and rescue himself.

2. A chief characteristic of psychic sleep is a false identity. A man labels himself in dozens of ways, then believes that these mere labels and words are real. We must rise above unconscious labels to realize our true nature.

3. Valuable self-knowledge comes through daily self-observation. Observe your thoughts and acts while neither praising nor condemning them, but simply to understand yourself.

4. Awareness of how our minds are conditioned is a power for breaking that conditioning. This results in a free and untroubled mind.

5. Take a new interest in your life by exploring these practical truths every day. They will prove themselves to you by providing a new life.

6. Use your human relations for inner-insight. Be conscious of the fear and confusion in men and women. Then know that *you* need not live like that.

Make up your mind to live your own life.

7. Realize that freedom is always personal and inward. As we free ourselves from our old and habitual nature, we are set free from its anxieties.

8. Remember the existence within you of a power which is never disturbed by anyone or anything. Your walk along the esoteric path brings you closer and closer to this power.

9. The person who commands himself will command all of life. This new command appears when we deeply realize our oneness with all of life.

10. Be your own teacher. Don't let others tell you what is right for you. The person who asks a question is quite capable of finding the answer within himself.

11. You are not chained to the past. You are free *right now* to live spontaneously and happily.

12. Be receptive to esoteric truths, especially to those which seem unusual to you at first. Remember, a new life can come only through a new understanding.

"WHEREFORE BE YE NOT UNWISE BUT UNDERSTANDING WHAT THE WILL OF THE LORD IS." EPH. 5:17

BEHOLD, ALL YE THAT KINDLE A FIRE AND WALK IN THE LIGHT OF YOUR FIRE. WHO IS THERE AMONG YOU THAT WALKETH IN DARKNESS AND HATH NO LIGHT? LET HIM TRUST IN THE LORD AND STAY UPON HIS GOD.

ISAIAH 50: 10,11

In Conclusion

Let nothing stop you from traveling the esoteric path to a new life. Let nothing stand in your way, not past mistakes, nor discouraging circumstances, nor other people, nor feelings of despair.

What now appears to be a brick wall will someday dissolve before your very eyes, before the eyes of your elevated understanding. One by one you will walk straight through the open spaces where the walls once seemed to be. The walls existed in your mind. But now you have a new mind so the road ahead is open all the way.

March forward with determination and good cheer. First you will sight your home, then you will reach home.

****

Vernon Howard broke through to another world. He saw through the illusion of suffering and fear and loneliness. From 1965 until his death in 1992 he wrote books and conducted classes which reflect a degree of skill and understanding that may be unsurpassed in modern history. Tape recordings of many of his class talks are available.

Today more than 8 million readers worldwide enjoy his exceptionally clear and inspiring presentations of the great truths of the ages. His books are widely used by doctors, psychiatrists, psychologists, counselors, clergymen, educators and people from all walks of life. All his teachings center around the one grand theme: *"There is a way out of the human problem and anyone can find it."*

march 16, 1918

august 23, 1992   74

PISCES

Other Writings by
VERNON HOWARD

****

Psycho-Pictography

The Power of Esoterics

A Treasury of Trueness

Pathways to Perfect Living

The Mystic Masters Speak

Mystic Path to Cosmic Power

Treasury of Positive Answers

50 Ways to See Thru People

50 Ways to Escape Cruel People

The Power of Your Supermind

Conquer Anxiety and Frustration

Your Power of Natural Knowing

700 Inspiring Guides to a New Life

Women—50 Ways to See Thru Men

Practical Exercises For Inner Harmony

Esoteric Encyclopedia of Eternal Knowledge

And Many Others

NEW LIFE FOUNDATION

****

New Life is a nonprofit organization founded by Vernon Howard in the 1970's for the distribution and dissemination of his teachings. It is for anyone who has run out of his own answers and has said to himself, "There has to be something else." These teachings *are* the something else. All are encouraged to explore and apply these profound truths—*they work!*

The Foundation conducts classes on a regular basis throughout Arizona, Colorado and Southern California. They are an island of sanity in a confused world. The atmosphere is friendly, light and uplifting. Don't miss the opportunity to attend your first New Life class.

For details on books, tapes and classes write:

Headquarters
NEW LIFE FOUNDATION
PO Box 2230
Pine, Arizona 85544
(520) 476-3224

Web: www.anewlife.org
E-mail: info@anewlife.org
Vernon Howard, Founder